D1243142

Distinctions in Nature

Deciduous Trees and Coniferous Trees Explained

Alicia Z. Klepeis

Cavendish Square
New York

Published in 2017 by Cavendish Square Publishing, LLC
243 5th Avenue, Suite 136, New York, NY 10016

Copyright © 2017 by Cavendish Square Publishing, LLC

First Edition

CPSIA Compliance Information: Batch #CS16CSQ

All websites were available and accurate when this book was sent to press.

Library of Congress Cataloging-in-Publication Data

Names: Klepeis, Alicia, 1971- author.
Title: Deciduous trees and coniferous trees explained / Alicia Z. Klepeis.
Description: New York : Cavendish Square Publishing, [2017] | Series: Distinctions in nature | Includes index.
Identifiers: LCCN 2015050834 (print) | LCCN 2016002503 (ebook)
ISBN 9781502617699 (pbk.) | ISBN 9781502617439 (library bound)
ISBN 9781502617569 (6 pack) | ISBN 9781502617484 (ebook)
Subjects: LCSH: Trees-Juvenile literature. | Conifers-Juvenile literature.
Classification: LCC QK475.8 .K578 2017 (print) | LCC QK475.8 (ebook)
DDC 582.16-dc23
LC record available at http://lccn.loc.gov/2015050834

Editorial Director: David McNamara
Editor: Kelly Spence
Copy Editor: Nathan Heidelberger
Art Director: Jeffrey Talbot
Designer: Stephanie Flecha
Production Assistant: Karol Szymczuk
Photo Research: J8 Media

The photographs in this book are used by permission and through the courtesy of: del.Monaco/Shutterstock.com, cover left; Leonid Ikan/Shutterstock.com, cover right; Bjorn Forsberg/Photolibrary/Getty Images, 4 left; Alexander Mazurkevich/Shutterstock.com, 4 right; VisitBritain/Britain on View/Britain On View/Getty Images, 6; Michael Shake/Shutterstock.com, 7; Anselm Schwietzke/EyeEm/Getty Images, 8; De Agostini Picture Library/De Agostini/Getty Images, 10; Dorling Kindersley/Getty Images, 11 bottom row; Dole08/Thinkstock, 11 top row; Peter Turner Photography/Shutterstock.com, 11 inset; Grigorii Pisotsckii/Shutterstock.com, 12; Whiteway/Shutterstock.com, 14; ES3N/iStock/Thinkstock, 15; John vlahidis/iStock/Thinkstock, 16; susandaniels/iStock/Thinkstock, 17 inset; Brian Maudsley/Shutterstock.com, 18; Stephen Dalton/Minden Pictures/Getty Images, 19; John Block/Photolibrary/Getty Images, 20 right; DEA/C. SAPPA/De Agostini Picture Library/Getty Images, 20 left; Christopher Gallagher/Photolibrary/Getty Images, 22 right; Brian Stablyk/Photographer's Choice RF/Getty Images, 22 left; IDAK/Shutterstock.com, 24; Mark Conlin/Oxford Scientific/Getty Images, 26 left; Tayakato/iStock/Thinkstock, 26 right; jadimages/Shutterstock.com, 27.

Printed in the United States of America

Contents

Trees provide homes for many
animals, like this fieldfare
sitting on its nest.

Ripe red apples are a tasty
snack for many different
animals.

Introduction: A Nature Walk

Take a walk outside. Can you spot a tree? Trees are plants. They are found all over the world and on every **continent** except Antarctica. All trees share some things in common. Every tree has a trunk, branches, and leaves. They also have roots that grow deep into the ground.

Many Tasks

Trees do many jobs. They provide homes for animals. Birds, bugs, monkeys, and squirrels are just a few animals that live in trees. Trees also produce **oxygen**, which all people need to breathe. They also help remove pollution from the air. Some trees even grow foods like apples or walnuts.

Classifying Trees

All trees share some characteristics. They can also be different from each other in many ways. Some trees lose their leaves each autumn. Others stay green all year long. Some trees have flowers. Others grow **cones**.

The green needles and cones of this pine tree are covered in snow during the winter.

The bright pink blossoms of a crabapple tree stand out against the sky on a sunny spring day.

A crabapple tree has beautiful pink blossoms in the spring. Pine trees grow cones instead of flowers.

There are tens of thousands of different kinds of trees found on the Earth. Scientists **classify** trees, or put them into different groups, based on their similarities. **Taxonomy** is the science of classifying **organisms**.

Orange and yellow leaves fall from deciduous maple trees as the weather cools in autumn.

1 Deciduous Trees and Coniferous Trees

Some trees lose their leaves each year. Have you ever seen a tree with bare branches in the winter? Then you have seen a **deciduous** tree. The word "deciduous" comes from a Latin word meaning "falling off." There are many kinds of deciduous trees. Hickory and apple trees are examples of deciduous trees.

Deciduous trees usually grow in places with warm summers and cold winters. The leaves of many deciduous trees change color in the fall. Maple leaves can turn orange, red, or yellow. In the United States, most deciduous trees lose their leaves when the weather turns colder. New leaves grow in the spring.

The Norway spruce is the traditional Christmas tree in homes throughout Europe. Its cones are among the largest in the spruce family.

Forever Green

Unlike deciduous trees, most **coniferous** trees, also known as conifers, do not lose their leaves each year. They stay green all year long. People sometimes call these trees **evergreens**. Coniferous trees usually have **needles** instead of big leaves. These needles can be sharp or soft to touch. Coniferous trees usually grow in places with short summers and long, snowy winters.

The word "coniferous" means "cone-bearing." All coniferous trees have cones. Pine and fir trees are both coniferous species. So are most Christmas trees, like the Norway spruce. The cones of coniferous trees contain seeds. New trees sprout from these seeds.

Zoom In

The monkey puzzle tree is native to South America. It has strange leaves and unusual-looking cones. It is a conifer.

Top: The cones of coniferous trees come in many shapes and sizes.

Bottom: These leaf cuttings from fir, spruce, and pine trees show how conifer leaves vary in color and texture.

The Colorado blue spruce has silvery, blue-green needles. Animals such as deer often eat these needles.

2 Comparing Deciduous Trees and Coniferous Trees

Deciduous and coniferous trees are different in lots of ways. One way to tell these trees apart is by looking at their leaves.

Different Kinds of Leaves

Conifers often have long, thin leaves called needles. The leaf of a Colorado blue spruce is pointed and sharp. It looks like a sewing needle.

Coniferous leaves are small and tough. A waxy **cuticle**, or outer layer, protects these

The Persian ironwood tree has egg-shaped leaves that will turn golden yellow, crimson, maroon, rose pink, or purple in autumn.

needlelike leaves from losing too much water. They also contain a special chemical that protects the needles from being damaged by frost during cold weather.

The evergreen leaves of conifers allow them to make food anytime there is enough sunlight. **Photosynthesis** is the process by which plants collect energy from the sun and turn it into fuel. This fuel helps the tree grow and reproduce.

The leaves of deciduous trees come in many shapes and sizes. Some, like maple tree leaves, are called **palmate**. This means they are shaped like a hand. Other deciduous tree leaves grow in different shapes. The Persian ironwood tree has egg-shaped leaves.

Deciduous trees' leaves are thin and flat. They have a much thinner cuticle than conifer leaves. The leaves on a deciduous tree can be easily damaged by frost, wind, and snow. Each autumn, deciduous trees in most parts of the United States drop their leaves. Oak, beech, and elm trees stand bare all winter. The **nutrients** from the fallen leaves **enrich** the soil around the trees. This helps the trees grow.

During the winter, deciduous trees become **dormant**. The trees survive off stored energy until the warm spring weather arrives.

Tree Shapes

Deciduous and coniferous trees often have different shapes. Many conifers have a **conical** shape. They look like upside-down ice cream cones. Branches at the top of a conifer are much shorter than those at the bottom.

A Japanese cedar tree's shape helps snow slide easily off its branches.

Zoom In

A pinecone is covered in small scales that protect the fragile seeds inside from cold or wet weather.

The conical shape is good for trees living in cold areas because snow falls easily off the branches. This protects the branches from breaking in the wintertime.

Many deciduous trees don't have a conical shape. They are wider and more spread out. The London plane tree is a large, broadly spreading tree. This broad design is helpful. The leaves on a deciduous tree are spread out, which allows them to take in as much sunlight as possible. The green leaves use the sunlight to make food. This helps the trees survive.

Growing up to 80 feet (24.4 meters) across, the London plane tree provides excellent shade.

Spreading Seeds

All trees produce seeds. New trees grow from these seeds. Many deciduous trees produce their seeds inside fruits. Conifers, like pine trees, grow their seeds inside cones. Coniferous trees are slow in producing their seeds. Male cones produce **pollen**. This pollen must reach the female cones to make a seed grow. New seeds then

Clouds of yellow pollen leave the male cones of an umbrella pine tree.

Deciduous Trees and Coniferous Trees Explained

grow and are protected inside the female cones. Pinecones are very hard. Cedar cones are softer and fall apart on the tree.

Coniferous and deciduous trees have different ways to spread their seeds. The cones of conifers open up in hot, dry weather. Then the seeds are released to begin their journey to becoming new trees.

Deciduous seeds travel in many ways. Maple seeds are found in cases, called keys, that spiral down to the ground like a helicopter. Oak seeds, located inside acorns, plop to the ground.

The key of a maple, containing the tree's seeds, spirals to the ground.

1. The Atlas cedar has barrel-shaped male cones that sit upright on the tree's lower branches. Its needles are somewhat stiff.

2. The American sycamore is a large, fast-growing tree with palmate leaves. After one year, these trees can reach up to 10 feet (3 m) in height.

3 Be a Tree Detective

Take a look at each photograph. Use the clues to figure out which trees (*left*) are deciduous and which ones are coniferous.

1. The Atlas cedar tree has barrel-shaped cones. The cones sit on top of the tree's branches. This tree is named after the Atlas Mountains in North Africa. Is this tree deciduous or coniferous? Why?

2. The American sycamore tree has hand-shaped leaves. These leaves are bright green in spring and summer. Then they turn brown in the fall. As the weather gets colder, these leaves fall off the tree. Is this a deciduous or coniferous tree? How can you tell?

3. A Douglas fir tree stands in Cathedral Grove, in British Columbia, Canada. Some of the trees found here are over eight hundred years old.

4. This Indian horse chestnut tree from the Himalayas produces magnificent flowers in early summer.

3. The Douglas fir has short, dark-green leaves. These narrow needles stay green all year long. They are protected by a waxy cuticle. Is this tree deciduous or coniferous? What qualities give this away?

Deciduous Trees and Coniferous Trees Explained

4. The horse chestnut tree is a tall, broadly shaped tree. It produces white and pink flowers each spring. These flowers turn into glossy, reddish-brown nuts called conkers. The conkers drop from the tree each autumn. Is this tree deciduous or coniferous? What clues help you decide?

Larch trees belong to the pine family. These trees grow mostly in cold areas in the northern hemisphere.

4 Rule Breakers

Not every tree on Earth falls neatly into the categories of coniferous or deciduous. Some are rule breakers.

Larch Trees

Some conifers are also deciduous. Say what? Yes, it's true. Larch trees, also called tamarack trees, have cones and needles. The needles of larch trees turn yellow in the fall. Then they fall off the trees. Each spring, new needles grow on the larch trees. These needles eventually darken and look like the other conifers' needles until the following autumn.

Around the World

Larch trees are not the only deciduous conifers. Deciduous conifers are found in many places around the world. The bald cypress tree is also a deciduous conifer. It

A stand of bald cypress trees grows in Lake Bradford, Florida. These trees can grow in wet or dry conditions.

The dawn redwood's needles change color and fall off the tree each autumn. This species has been around since the days when dinosaurs walked the Earth.

is native to the southeastern United States. The bald cypress can survive in freshwater **swamps**. It often grows in water that is 3 feet (1 m) or more deep. These trees drop their leaves each year.

Dawn redwoods are deciduous conifers that are native to China. Their leaves turn reddish or orange brown before falling off each year.

The next time you take a walk outside, look at the trees. Can you tell which are deciduous and which are coniferous?

Deciduous and coniferous trees are ablaze with color in autumn along the Blue Ridge Parkway in the eastern United States.

classify To arrange in or assign to categories based on shared characteristics.

cones The dry fruits of conifers, which often have rounded ends and contain the seeds of the tree.

conical Shaped like a cone.

coniferous Relating to a tree that bears cones and has needlelike or scalelike leaves.

continent One of the great divisions of land on Earth, such as North America or Asia.

cuticle A protective, waxy layer covering the epidermis of a plant.

deciduous Shedding its leaves annually, as of a tree or shrub.

dormant Describing being alive but not in an active state of growth.

enrich To make soil more fertile.

evergreens Plants that keep their green leaves all year long.

needles The stiff, slender, often sharp leaves of a conifer.

nutrients Substances that provide nourishment needed for growth and the maintenance of life.

organisms Individual plants, animals, or single-celled life-forms.

oxygen A colorless, odorless gas that is essential to the survival of living things.

palmate Resembling a hand with the fingers spread out.

photosynthesis The process by which green plants use sunlight to make food from carbon dioxide and water.

pollen A fine, powdery substance, usually yellow, that is made up of microscopic grains discharged from the male cone or part of a flower.

swamps Areas of wet, spongy land that are often partly covered by water.

taxonomy The orderly classification of plants and animals according to their natural relationships.

Find Out More

Books

Burnie, David. *Tree*. DK Eyewitness Books. New York: DK Publishing, 2015.

Hall, Katharine. *Trees: A Compare and Contrast Book*. Mount Pleasant, SC: Arbordale Publishing, 2014.

Ingoglia, Gina. *The Tree Book for Kids and Their Grown-Ups*. New York: Brooklyn Botanic Garden, 2013.

Websites

DK Findout! Deciduous Trees
www.dkfindout.com/us/animals-and-nature/plants/deciduous-trees
Read all about deciduous trees.

DK Findout! Evergreens
www.dkfindout.com/us/animals-and-nature/plants/evergreen-trees
Explore the features of coniferous trees.

Index

Page numbers in **boldface** are illustrations.

About the Author

Alicia Klepeis loves to research fun and out-of-the-ordinary topics that make nonfiction exciting for readers. Alicia began her career at the National Geographic Society. She is the author of many kids' books, including *The World's Strangest Foods*, *Bizarre Things We've Called Medicine*, *Francisco's Kites*, and *From Pizza to Pisa*. She lives with her family in upstate New York.

DATE DUE